JANE AUSTEN VISITS

In Memory of

Patricia Clarke

Chairman
Jane Austen London Group
1996-2006

'There were twenty Dances & I danced them all, & without any fatigue.'
(Letter to Cassandra, dated 24.12.1798)

JANE AUSTEN VISITS LONDON

Vera Quin

Cappella Archive
Book on Demand Editions

Cappella Archive : 2008

British Library Cataloguing-in-Publication Data
A catalogue record for this book is
available from the British Library

978–1–902918–46–4

Typeset by PostScript Markup
Cappella Archive : Great Malvern : WR14 4RQ
www.cappella-archive.com

Printed and Bound
Aspect Design : Great Malvern : WR14 1PD

Contents

First Impressions

IT IS a truth universally acknowledged that of Jane Austen's one hundred and sixty extant letters, thirty were written from London between 1796 and 1815. A little more counting will suggest that in her lifetime of forty-one years she left records of less than one full year in London, though she did stay or travel through the capital on some dozen other occasions. Yet this short period of her life generated nearly a fifth of her letters. What did she find in London that prompted her, in the middle of endless distractions to write these long, long letters, particular, immediate, urgent? That is their defining feature: what is said in them matters *now*, either because it concerns a complicated series of arrangements for coming or going, or meeting or avoiding people, or because something has been seen or done that must be shared at once. The news cannot wait. In London so much is going on, so much is vivid, pressing, important, so different in tempo from life in the country with its 'constant succession of small events'.

Yet the approach to London was, by our standards, very leisurely: a coach or a curricle, a stop for a meal but long enough to buy some gloves, perhaps a night on the way. Eventually the road swept over Kingston Bridge, through the turnpike gate by the Queen's Elm in Fulham Road and then veered right along Brompton Road. The penultimate stop before the terminus at Charing Cross was at the Knightsbridge Floor Cloth Factory. In this large building, on the site of Harvey Nichols, an early form of linoleum was made, with a side-line in large tents, much in demand during a quarter century of war. It was a prosperous enterprise, with landscaped forecourt, a rank of hackney coaches and it was the handiest getting off point for travellers bound for Chelsea, or its modern addition, Hans Town. Here Henry Austen, Jane's favourite brother, lived during his prosperous years, a witty, entertaining man who charmed everyone.

As the coach progressed eastward, into London proper, the houses were closer-packed and seemed to stretch indefinitely. For London, at a million inhabitants in 1800, was the largest city in Europe and in her novels and letters Jane Austen mentioned parts of it from Hendon in the north to Streatham in the south—both at the time outlying villages—and from Chelsea, the newly fashionable suburb in the west to Gracechurch Street within easy walking distance of the Tower at its eastern boundary. And over most of it hung a cloud of smoke.

Forget Wordsworth's 'All bright and glittering in the smokeless air'. He wrote very early on a summer's day, and besides poetic licence was his legitimate tool. Forget Canaletto, whose gentle curve of buildings along the Thames rears delicate spires into a blue Italianate sky. London burnt coal, and coal made smoke, as testified by many travellers, not least a scandalised Walter Scott comparing London to Paris in 1815.

Nearer the centre the traffic thickened, there were frequent accidents and caricatures of accidents. The pavements were crowded, street vendors cried their wares, dogs made use of lamp-posts, tavern doors and shop windows attracted knots of potential customers, deciding whether to go in or not. Round Charing Cross, overlooked by the familiar statue of Charles I protected by iron railings, the throng was heaviest and the air in the narrow streets smelliest. Here the extensive Royal Mews occupied a good portion of the present Trafalgar Square and at the start of the Strand stood the Golden Cross:

> 'an inn of very considerable business whence many coaches arrive and from whence many depart to all parts of the country'.

This coaching inn was flanked by stands of hackney coaches (there were 1100 of them in London in 1811), theoretically parked at 16ft intervals, to be picked up individually like taxis. Hackneys were allowed to pick up travellers only 'on the pavement', that is the paved areas which defined London's limits: obviously the City and the City of Westminster, but also Chelsea in the west and the area round Brunswick Square on the northern edge.

The Golden Cross and its neighbouring coaching inns did not form the only terminus. Piccadilly was a smaller one, with the most comfortable departure point in the capital on the site of the present Ritz. Ludgate Hill had La Belle Sauvage—starting point for Cambridge—and its satellites, full of passengers heading north. Cheapside boasted the Swan with Two Necks with underground stabling for two thousand horses. Specifically Gracechurch Street, home of Mr and Mrs Gardiner of *Pride and Prejudice*, had the Spread Eagle and the Cross Keys, catering for traffic to Kent, Dover and the continent. So when Wickham and Lydia elope from Brighton, it is astute of them to hunker down in the area (they were eventually married in St Clement's, the *Oranges and Lemons* church in Eastcheap, now King William Street). With forty-eight daily coach departures from four inns in the immediate vicinity, a newly arrived young couple would be unnoticeable.

That is unless they got into trouble with the law. But arrest of wrong-doers was less likely in the City, which had fewer and smaller police patrols than the rest of London, which was officially in Middlesex and the Middlesex Justices Act applied. This act of 1792 was brought in by Pitt against considerable opposition, even without the City merchants weighing in. The argument against it was that hanging and transportation to Australia (with the *Declaration of Independence* the former colonies in America could no longer be used as a dumping ground) were powerful deterrents; therefore policing should be at local, parish level, because a central system would endanger individual liberties.

However Pitt's government had its way and the new act set up seven new Police Offices, each with three salaried magistrates sitting daily and supported by six policemen with powers to arrest 'ill-disposed and suspected persons'. The patrol out of Bow Street was increased to seventy armed men. This was the court where John Fielding, the humane, blind magistrate and his half-brother the novelist Henry, had sat for many years. Privately commissioned constables or watchmen were common, for instance West Indian merchants had their own to minimise theft from their ships. After 1800, with the country at war, this was supported by another magistrates' court at 'Wapping New-Stairs for offences connected with shipping in the Port of London'. An 1805 guide to the capital gives a complete list 'as it is the highest importance to strangers to be able to obtain redress from the police, in case of injury'.

In her novels and letters Jane mentioned a considerable number of addresses 'on the pavement', also Hampstead, Hendon, Streatham, outlying villages accessible by local coach. There were six of these from Chelsea alone to various points in the centre. In general local coaches provided a service akin to modern bus routes, supplementing the long distance coaches. The latter could deposit incoming travellers at any stop on their route but could not take outgoing passengers from the centre just to their first stop. So if Jane was staying with Henry in Chelsea and wanted to go to stay with her brother Edward in Kent, she would have taken a hackney possibly to Gracechurch Street, boarded the Dover coach, rattled over London Bridge, through Dartford, Rochester, Sittingbourne to Canterbury. For Jane, London was a hub as well as a place to stay.

Jane's thirty London letters, mostly to her sister Cassandra, so even in their handwriting, so long to our e-mail sensitised eyes, so full of factual information, reveal little of herself. How irksome was her total dependence on her brothers for any movement beyond walking distance? Certainly in 1799 she gave up all thought of going to Kent with Charles, her youngest brother, because of 'the unpleasantness of returning by myself'. Did she long to buy something other than her modest purchases for dress? How much more time did she want to spend in London?

Writing from Kent in November 1813 she made no bones about inviting herself to visit Henry, her London-based favourite brother: 'it will be a great pleasure to be with him, as it always is'. She wanted to negotiate the publication of *Mansfield Park* with Thomas Egerton, her usual publisher, so 'I will stay with him (ie Henry) let it be ever so disagreeable to him'. In the event, in less than a week brother Edward, her host in Kent, escorted her back home to Chawton.

She is personally the most elusive of writers and London, the great capital extravagantly heaving with life, encourages a number of unwarranted suppositions. The text of her letters, period guide books, itineraries, maps, directories, play bills, leases, rent books provide the facts. When a theory is a theory you will, dear reader, be told. But there are distinct gaps for your imagination to fill, as you will shortly discover.

1796

JANE'S first letter from London is dated 'Tuesday 23 August 1796, Cork Street', a short street on the Burlington Estate, today accessed by walking up from Piccadilly through the Burlington Arcade. At its other end is Cork Street, now awash with galleries, then strictly residential, with houses continuous on its west side backing on to New Bond Street.

At the start of the twenty-first century three period buildings in New Bond Street still give a good idea of what it was like in 1796. The largest, numbers 34 and 35 is Sotheby's, then a pub (it still has a café) with extensive stables, now the auction house that started in the Strand in 1744 and moved to New Bond Street in 1917. Two jewellers, Lucy Campbell at number 26 and Bentley & Skinner at number 8, have preserved their original shop fronts and interior proportions, that is they have not expanded backwards to take in their courtyards. So these houses are shallow, very obviously at number 8 which, in the eighteenth century, backed on to stables servicing Cork Street. The east side of this was largely undeveloped, that is bordered by walls overhung by trees from gardens in the parallel Old Burlington Street. There the houses were larger than in Cork Street, occupied about equally by titled and medical men, with the odd retired soldier and the Duke of Devonshire's agent spreading himself over two houses.

Cork Street was more colourful. At No. 1 lived Sir Robert Mackreth, described as 'club proprietor, began life as a billiard marker'. He moved on into money-lending, was taken to court for defrauding a minor, involved in an attempted duel and ended in prison. On the way his neighbour in New Burlington Street, Horace Walpole, son of the Prime Minister, collector and letter writer, was furious with his own elder brother for nominating Mackreth for a pocket borough in his gift. But despite—or because of—all the distinctly shady activities Mackreth was involved in, he was MP, knighted by George III and died possessed of the house in Cork Street, an estate near Southampton, another in the Lake District and a West Indian plantation. A self-made man, but not one for Jane to socialise with.

Nor was Thomas Penstone, a hairdresser, who occupied two houses, nor Richard Seccombe, the upholsterer, who lived in a large house, annual rent of £85. The most expensive and largest house was in the name of Dr Alex Mayersbach, who had inherited a fortune built on a quack medicine consisting mostly of urine. Joyce Booth, occupation unstated, was in the next house, and the one on her other side was let out to tenants. Two separate houses and a stable unit in the mews at the back are labelled as belonging to 'Squire Stapleton'—no Christian name. The supposition, supported by plausible local evidence, is that this was Lord Morley of Saltram who, as the guide book to that beautiful Adam House has it, 'had relationships with women other than his wives, notably Lady Elizabeth Monck' the reputedly exceptionally beautiful, 'daughter of the Earl of Arran, by whom he had three sons'. The boys were given the surname Stapleton. It sounds as if his London love nest was in Cork Street, with the second house—and both were small—as a separate nursery wing. This would not be worth mentioning were it not for one curious fact: twenty years on, when the bankrupt Henry Austen was living on a curate's stipend of 52 guineas a year. Lord Morley threw him a mini life-line by appointing him as chaplain to the family in Devon. Presumably sometime earlier their paths had usefully crossed.

Numbers 15 and 16, two of the smallest houses, were occupied by George Robinson, another hairdresser, the next equally small one by General Vernon. The last one on the west side was marginally larger and 'Benj. Langlois Esq.' paid rent of £40 a year.

Benjamin Langlois had been on the staff of the British Embassy in Rome, and MP and Under-Secretary, in short a public man who knew what was needed and what to be avoided if a man was to make for himself a position and a reputation in the world. He had helped one nephew, the Rev. George Lefroy, to the parish of Ashe, next to Steventon, Jane's birthplace, and was now concentrating on a great-nephew from Ireland, a biddable young man named Tom Lefroy. Tom wanted to study law in London, living with his uncle the while (where better?) but first went to stay with his uncle and aunt in Ashe. He met Jane Austen, who obviously found him attractive, and she decided to have a fling.

There is remarkably little genuine evidence about this episode, on which any number of extrapolations, in print and on screen, have been built. Suffice it to say that the flirtation, with Jane setting the pace, was brief and judging by her letters, hugely enjoyable. Their elders separated them soon enough. ('Do not involve your self in an affection which the want of fortune would make so very imprudent'). Or perhaps Tom just had to get back to London for the start of term. But while it lasted, for Jane, the excitement had been palpable; the flutter in the sentences describing their few encounters is unmistakable. The flirtation had provided material for gossip and Cassandra had written a scolding letter. Undeterred Jane swept on:

> 'Imagine to yourself everything most profligate and shocking in the way of dancing and sitting down together. I can expose myself, however, only once more, because he leaves the country soon after next Friday, on which we are to have a dance at Ashe after all.'

Five days later, she was still at it:

> 'At length the Day is come on which I am to flirt my last with Tom Lefroy, & when you receive this it will be over.'

Now, seven months later, there is one brief letter and one only, with the same flutter. Dated from Cork Street, it shows she had come up with two brothers, Edward the landowner, and Frank, the elder of the two sailor brothers.

Edward had immediately gone on to his home in Kent, Frank off to hunt for tickets for the evening show at Astley's. This was the recently rebuilt Amphitheatre of the Arts, on the Lambeth side of

Westminster Bridge; it had been decorated 'by a Scotch artist' to imitate a woodland grove and offered equestrian events, songs, musical interludes, acrobats. The theory, for which there is no evidence, is that Jane had come to London to see Tom and be looked over by old uncle Benjamin Langlois. If he approved, an official engagement to Tom might follow. Jane probably wanted it, but Tom? A miniature shows him with a hesitant, half-defensive smile, a mild, guileless face, at odds with period portraits of young officers, their schooled aggression totally under control, or portraits of young dilettanti, whose attentive eyes are evaluating the latest connoisseur's bauble. A dear boy, but not a risk taker, and marrying a penniless girl of coruscating intelligence would be plain dangerous.

The immediate question is: in August 1796 where was Jane staying while she was in Cork Street? It was not with Henry, with whom she often stayed later; in 1796 he was still with the Oxford Militia stationed in East Anglia. The obvious answer is at uncle Benjamin's house, 18 Cork Street. But the house was small, one of the five smallest in the row and Mrs Lefroy, the young man's aunt, declares categorically in two letters of January 1803 that there is no space for a visiting woman, even one travelling with her husband. After all it was a bachelor establishment for uncle Benjamin and young Tom. Also, had Jane stayed in the house, who would have chaperoned her? A young girl staying alone in the house of her boy-friend and his uncle would certainly not have been acceptable before World War I, let alone a hundred years earlier, and would raise eyebrows in some quarters even now. Would Jane, bereft of all worldly advantages, or her parents, have allowed her reputation to be even mildly questioned? If she did indeed stay in the house unchaperoned, her very willingness to do so may have militated against her in uncle Benjamin's eyes. In the event, (and this is backed by hard evidence) within a twelve month Tom chose an unimpeachable bride, daughter of a baronet and heiress of an Irish pile still listed in 1950 *Gazetteer of the British Isles*.

But Jane would have been hurt straight away, in August 1796. Perhaps she took her hurt out walking, looking at the houses of the prosperous and estimating the precise social layer its occupiers hailed from, starting with an easy one, in near-by Grosvenor Street for the estate-less Mr and Mrs Hurst of *Pride and Prejudice*. With the first version of *Sense and Sensibility* in mind, she calibrated Park Street for the very wealthy Mrs Ferrars, Hanover Square and Conduit Street for Mrs Jennings' well-settled daughters (in modern jargon, they had married up), Mrs Jennings somewhat less well-placed near Portman Square, and John and Fanny Dashwood in boring Harley Street. Did she get as far as Bartlett Buildings off Fleet Street, the temporary perch of the impecunious Steele sisters?

One way or another, she was probably licking her wounds and thinking of other wounded girls, Marianne Dashwood for one, traditionally written into life the year before. The memory of her brief jubilant happiness would be fed into *First Impressions* (later *Pride and Prejudice*) to be started within months; the hurt would be recalled in her last completed book: Anne Elliot carried her pain without complaint, making the best of her given life. As did Jane, who was whisked away to stay with Edward's young family. The early autumn was sunny and hot, visitors numerous, outings frequent. It sounds very cheerful, at least on the surface, which is all Jane ever allows herself to describe. The stop-over in Cork Street remains unmentioned. In future London will be the place for professional advancement and entertainment.

1811

AFTER 1801 the Austen family's London base was with Henry, Jane's favourite brother, who had married his widowed first cousin, Eliza de Feuillide and set up as a banker. Jane's letters, describing her longer and important visits to London start in 1811, in that year from 64 Sloane Street, a large house appropriate to the status of a rising banker and his dashing wife. Staying with Henry and Eliza was fun. Both were highly gregarious, loved parties, the theatre, being in the swim. People by the dozen were seen every week, and even if they were bores they merited a mention to her sister Cassandra, often with an unflattering adjective or phrase attached. Being 'judgmental' was not then the sin that it has since become. Nowadays their names for the most part mean nothing except to their descendants or local historians, but they crowd Jane's London horizon, filling it with energy and variety. Of course she came to London in the first instance for a serious purpose, or rather two of them. The first was to parley with a publisher, previously identified by Henry, about how her next book was to see the light of day, or having done so, to correct the proofs. The second and very time-consuming one was shopping.

The shops were mostly in two sets of streets, running roughly parallel, with some overlap. The northern set was from Shoreditch Church to Bishopsgate, Threadneedle Street, Cheapside, Newgate, Holborn and St Giles to Oxford Street. The shorter and 'most splendid' southern line started in Whitechapel, went on to Leadenhall Street, Cheapside, St Paul's Churchyard, Ludgate Street, Fleet Street, the Strand to Charing Cross. This arrangement was highly satisfactory for the majority, who lived east of Charing Cross, not so good for the wealthier and more fashion-conscious inhabitants of Mayfair, developed only since the middle of the eighteenth century. For them there were additional shops in the transverse streets stretching from the main arteries. So dealers in luxuries, like Wedgwood or Sheraton were near their clientèle in St James's. Bond Street was a recognised shopping street, visited repeatedly by Jane, either for her own purchases, or with her niece Fanny for instance seeking sheet music at Robert Birchall's at number 135.

A trifle downmarket Golden Square in Soho housed Broadwood the piano makers, who seem also to have disappeared, although their instruments are still to be found. Not that Jane was after household goods, unless tea comes into that category, from R.J., R.G., and T.A. Twining 'tea men to Her Majesty' in the Strand. What she sought was fabrics.

Here London was far better supplied than Bath or Southampton, her earlier hunting grounds. London drapers also brought several improvements to selling. The invention of plate glass allowed larger panes of glass to be made, which led to shop windows with fewer glazing bars and therefore better visibility. Also the fabrics, displayed hanging from a specific shop fitment, could be judged how they would look made up into a dress, and so more readily assessed, compared, admired. To increase their impact shopkeepers often installed and maintained at their own expense bright lights trained on their windows. This had the secondary advantage of making shopping streets much brighter than residential ones, at least until about 10 p.m. Since shopkeepers often lived above their shops they could keep them open, with lights on, as long as they liked.

Fabrics were bought in dress lengths, so the phrase 'I got my Mother's gown' refers to the material only. The width of the fabric was obviously relevant and it should have been either an ell ($1\frac{1}{4}$ yards = 45 inches = 114 cm) or half an ell. Sometimes the manufacturers cheated and produced fabric no wider than $19\frac{1}{2}$ inches, which may not have been discovered until the fabric was unpacked at home. This might then necessitate a change in the pattern of the dress, 'some contrivance may be necessary' as Jane realised in April 1811.

Jane was after dimity, a cotton usually undyed, with a raised pattern; poplins, either a mixture of silk and wool or a cotton with a corded surface; Irish, a type of linen; kerseymere, a fine closely woven wool; sarsanet, a light silk; worsted; purl ribbon, something like a ribbon with a fringe, a temporary craze. She bought stockings, handkerchiefs, gloves. The last were about the only item from which tax was removed in Jane's lifetime, so when in *Emma* Frank Churchill buys a pair at Ford's he is not spreading himself. She went shopping with Fanny, her niece, or Eliza, her sister-in-law, or a maid, for ladies did not go to the shops alone, never after dark and never carried their purchases home—shops delivered. She went to a variety of drapers, looking specifically for 'a check'd Muslin', yielded to temptation to buy 'pretty coloured muslins' —while an elegant grey and white check features in the standard source book for the period Barbara Johnson's *Album of Styles and Fashions*.

At 35 she presumably considered herself too young for a darkish colour, for she went on to buy another patterned with 'a small red spot' for Cassandra, her senior by two years. These were found at Grafton House, on the corner of Bond and Grafton Streets. This much frequented shop was liable to very slow service, as Jane discovered on her several return visits, once walking there from Henrietta Street 'to get that over before breakfast'. The delay was complained of repeatedly in the letters and used to good narrative purpose in *Sense and Sensibility*, when Elinor has to wait while the foppish Robert Ferrars makes up his mind over the design of his toothpick case.

Shops, shoppers, theatre audiences, people visited or visiting all provided a panorama of changing fashions and Jane's beady eye for detail leads to frequent and lengthy comments. On the printed page there is much more about fashion than about the theatre, the topic identified as being of prime interest to her as a novelist. Perhaps information about fashion was impatiently awaited at Chawton, so that a clever alteration to a dress—with help from a shop in

Alton or a travelling haberdasher—could achieve a subtle move in one-up-manship. Jane writes at length about caps, made for Fanny or herself to new patterns, with a variety of trimmings. She made an effort by 'trying to draw up . . . black satin ribbon with proper perl edge . . . into kind of Roses, instead of putting it in plain double pleats' to refresh a dress, or 'lowered the bosom especially at the corners' of another. The growing acceptability of long sleeves for the evening was noted step by step. Jane also noted in 1814 'Waists short . . . the Bosom covered', 'Veils . . . upon several vulgar heads' and was relieved when corsets were altered so that the 'Bosom is not worn so high'. In September 1814 she described in detail 'the present style of female dress' as seen in the streets and in drawing rooms: 'the coloured petticoats with braces over white Spencers and enormous bonnets'.

Skirts had generally shortened during the war years, perhaps to use less fabric, a form of saving in an inflationary period. The fashion for simple, straight dressed in the Greek 'naked' style used less fabric than the earlier fuller skirts and elaborately flounced sleeves. Separation from the continent by war led to an insular style of dress developing, especially with the waning influence of Rose Bertin. This accomplished lady, Queen Marie Antoinette's dressmaker and hairdresser, had been an early émigrée to London. So by the time English tourists visited the continent again in 1814, their clothes were considered appalling. The shortness of their skirts made them look like tight-rope walkers, and their sheath dresses, with deep decolletés, were indecently tight. Jane retained a close eye for fashion to the end, writing three weeks before her death of a naval friend's 'wife and sister all good humour and obligingness and I hope (since fashion allows it) with rather longer petticoats than last year'. With the war over, continental fashions were making a comeback.

Only three of Jane's extant letters of the year 1811 were written from London, or more precisely Chelsea, in those days officially in the county of Middlesex, at 64 Sloane Street. Here publication of

Sense and Sensibility and *Pride and Prejudice* was planned and some proofs corrected.

The house, together with those in the adjoining streets, was part of the Hans Town development. The architect Henry Holland, who designed for the Prince Regent the first version of Royal Pavilion in Brighton, had taken a long lease on 100 acres of land belonging to Lord Cadogan, acquired by the latter through a far-sighted marriage. The land was open, bordered to the north-west by nurseries supplying vegetables and flowers for London proper, that is east of Park Lane. Holland kept twenty-one acres on the edge of the village for himself and built something like a manor house called variously Sloane Place or the Pavilion. The house was big enough to hold a drawing office beside a suite of fine rooms, and complete with stables, coach-house, laundry, ice-house, dove-cot, pig sties and dung heap.

The south front overlooked gardens and park landscaped by Holland's father-in-law, Capability Brown. Apart from 'a fine sheet of water', there were flower-beds, 'a considerable variety of fanciful intricate paths and scenery', shrubberies, grass, cows, sheep and sundry new-built ruins rendered picturesque by 'the appearance of age and decay', a feature noted in the guide books of the period. (Twentieth century guide-books suggest the effect was achieved by using stones from Cardinal Wolsey's house in Esher.) On the north side, the colonnaded entrance front faced the most ambitious part of the new development: Hans Place, a rectangle with the corners cut off and several openings. The east side was edged by the nascent Sloane Street.

While Holland limited himself to developing only part of the 79 acres left for private housing, he sub-let chunks of the site to other builders, with the proviso that his design had to be followed throughout. This was partly for aesthetic reasons and more immediately because the 1774 London Building Act had added Chelsea to the Cities of London and Westminster and so extended west the metropolitan building regulations that his plans had fully taken into account. Any infringement would have jeopardised the profitability of the enterprise. The houses were to be of moderate size, with no bow windows or projections, only door-cases and iron rails. The bricks to be used were made of gault clay from Cambridgeshire, of an unusual pale beige-grey, startling enough for the finished blocks of houses (basement, mezzanine, and two floors above) to be initially described as 'white cliffs'. However the bricks soon discoloured and turned an agreeable pale brown still to be seen on the lower floors of 30 Hans Place. Some of the early occupiers gave their houses a white lime wash to preserve the distinctive original pallor. Others gave up the struggle and chose a black wash instead. This explains why the only one of the original houses left, 123 Sloane Street, is now black, a slice of urban elegance akin to a Chanel suit in a gaggle of dowdy women.

The Hans Town development had a sewer, its own powers over paving, street cleaning and lighting, repairs and its own watchmen; in short it was a desirable residential area on the edge of the capital. Chelsea had also improved: Ranelagh pleasure gardens with its Rotunda and pavilions went out of fashion and grew disreputable before closing in 1805. The Swann Inn on the Embankment now had an adjacent brewery. The regular Chelsea Coach from the White Horse at the foot of Church Street—itself an enclave of quiet professional families—and a hackney stand by the Royal Hospital ensured easy access to Westminster and the City. Sloane Square, a stretch of grass surrounded with wooden posts and chains, was the site where Queen Charlotte's Royal Volunteers often assembled and then, with band playing, marched up Sloane Street, past the School of Industry for Girls. This was an establishment which, for the entry price of 2 guineas each, annually trained 50 young girls in the domestic crafts, that is made them employable as a better class of domestic servant. To the west of Sloane Street 1811 saw the building of the Roman Catholic chapel of St Mary. The Duchesse d'Angoulème, daughter of the guillotined king Louis XVI, laid the foundation stone, an émigré abbé designed it and it cost all of £6,000. There were fewer footpads between Hyde Park Gate and Kensington and the infamous Swann Inn at Knightsbridge had disappeared some years earlier.

Henry's house in Sloane Street faced east, across gardens. Its most attractive feature was the first floor, approached by a broad staircase giving on to a wide landing between the east-facing front drawing room and an octagonal drawing room (was it intended to echo Hans Place?) at the back. It was here on a hot evening in April that Eliza gave her music party and Jane, in London to correct the proofs of *Sense and Sensibility*, was one of the sixty-six attending it. She spent most of the evening on the landing 'which was comparatively cool' and had two extra benefits: 'the music at a pleasant distance as well as the first view of every new comer'.

This last was something of a habit with Jane. The story is told that whenever she spent the day in her brother Edward's Tudor mansion on the edge of Chawton, the village she lived in after 1809, her favourite spot was in the alcove overlooking the drive up to the house. Also when in 1815 she stayed with Henry in his largest house on the corner of Hans Place, she chose for herself the attic bedroom, overlooking the front door. Was this the novelist's instinct for the traditional trigger of a story: one or more incomers to a settled community start the action rolling?

Think about it: every one of her novels, including *The Watsons* and *Sanditon* starts precisely in this way. Be that as it may, the party was deemed a great success and was noted in the *Morning Post* of 25 April 1811, presumably to Eliza's satisfaction.

She had worked hard to make it the success it undoubtedly was, 'walking out by herself' ('a glass for the Mantelpiece', that is a mirror, had to be found in a hurry) and 'a good dose of Walking and Coaching' with Jane, who does not complain, although she had a few days earlier walked with Manon, the maidservant, from Sloane Street to Grafton House, on the corner of 164 Bond Street and Grafton Street, that is nearer Piccadilly than Oxford Street. And then she had to wait 'a full half hour before we could be attended to'. She does not mention how irritating she found the customers in the queue ahead of her.

Nor does she mention the route she took. As she turned right at the top of Sloane Street, the Royal Castle public house was just west of Knightsbridge, literally a bridge over the Westbourne, the stream that still drains the Serpentine; it then meandered through open ground east of Sloane Street (nowadays it is enclosed in a pipe), to end eventually in the Thames. Generally a docile stream the Westbourne had spectacularly overflowed in 1809, turned the Knightsbridge area into a lake and given a bonanza to Thames watermen, who for several days rowed foot passengers to and from Chelsea. Consequently the modern paving extended only along Knightsbridge Terrace, a stretch of some 40 small houses, the road was dimly lit by oil lamps, the protection of the citizenry left to the resident soldiers: barracks usually occupied by Guards regiments were heavy brick buildings spaced around an oblong parade ground. These were for the soldiers. An extra wing at the west end housed officers and a riding school, and a further open 'amphitheatre' at the back provided more space for exercising horses.

The ground rose to Hyde Park Gate corner, the slope of the roadway covered in gravel. Did she cut through the south-east tip of Hyde Park (where Apsley House, later known as Number 1 London was not yet built) and into Mayfair from Park Lane? Or she could have walked down Piccadilly as far as Bond Street, and on the way past the long reservoir running by the edge of Green Park. These details were probably familiar and therefore not worth mentioning to Cassandra, to whom the bulk of the London letters were written and, on the available evidence, Jane is not exactly an enthusiast for changing townscapes: they seldom surface in the novels and always for a purpose.

The 'coaching' done with Eliza would have been in a hackney, the equivalent of a taxi. This could have been picked up at one of the 18 official coach stands listed, or as it was returning empty to its stand. Hackney coachmen were 'obliged every day of the week to go to any place within ten miles if he has time to return by sunset', easy enough in April even before daylight saving was thought of. The charges were determined by the Commissioners of the Coach Office; Sloane Street to Grafton House would have cost 1/6 (one shilling and sixpence) too much for Jane's slender funds but manageable for Eliza, especially when she was hurrying to get the house ready for the music party.

Over and above all the guests at Eliza's party, Jane enjoyed meeting people on more intimate occasions, 'I find these little parties very pleasant', for instance Mr and Mrs Tilson—he was Henry's partner in the bank—who often crop up in the letters written from London. A more exotic family were the Comte and Comtesse d' Antraigues—she was a former opera singer—and their son. The father hailed from near Bordeaux, where Eliza's first French husband had also had his estates. So she may well have met him, in the country or in Paris.

Eliza would certainly have heard of him, for he was one of the leaders of the aristocrats' party, which at the start of the Revolution of 1789 had the limited aim of depriving the King of his absolute power. However the party was rapidly outmanoeuvred by the extremists, d'Antraigues fled and re-invented himself as a diplomat for any country opposed to republican and later Napoleonic France. In fact he was a spy; after various vicissitudes he fetched up in London in 1807 where Canning, then Foreign Secretary, offered him the post of Director of British Intelligence.

This was turned down although d'Antraigues continued working unofficially for British Intelligence and the family were prominent members of the numerous French emigration. Eliza hoped they would come to her party. They excused themselves, but asked Eliza, Henry and Jane to visit them just before. The journey however was not altogether smooth:

> 'the Horses actually gibbed on this side of Hyde Park Gate—a load of fresh gravel made it a formidable hill for them and they refused the collar.'

CHELSEA AND KNIGHTSBRIDGE

But eventually the Austens got there, probably a house in the rectangle edged by Marylebone Road (new at the time), Portman Street, Oxford Street and Harley Street, where the most prosperous of the French émigrés had their town residence. The d'Antraigues had:

> 'some fine paintings, which delighted Henry—and among them a Miniature of Philip V of Spain, Louis XIV's Grandson, which exactly suited my capacity'.

Did Jane's 'capacity' lead her to prefer small areas of paint, like her 'little piece of ivory'? Or remind her that Philip V had been forced to cede Gibraltar to the British, which, a century later, made the Austen sailor brothers' lives that much easier? Or was she interested only in portraits?

The theme of facial features being a good guide to character had been elaborated by John Caspar Lavater's three volumes of *Essays on Physiognomy designed to promote Knowledge and Love of Mankind* (1789-98) to quite subtle variations of character. Portraits can be stared at without rudeness, so Catherine Morland, as a polite guest, can ask to see a portrait of Mrs Tilney, Elizabeth Bennet can pause in front of 'a striking resemblance' of Mr Darcy, both girls seeking the mind's construction in the face. As a novelist Jane was interested in the first without ever describing the second.

A Sunday walk in Kensington Gardens with Henry and two of his friends was an opportunity to notice the lilacs in bloom, the horse chestnuts 'quite out—everything was fresh and beautiful'. On another day with Mary (unidentified) Jane went to the Liverpool Museum, in Piccadilly. This was a collection of natural curiosities and had first been shown in Liverpool. Transferring to London in 1809 it rapidly became a highly fashionable place of entertainment, in short a place to be seen. While they were about it the two young women—young at least by current standards, Jane being only 35—they walked a little further, to the British Gallery in Pall Mall. This housed a commercial show run by the British Institution, the directors of which:

'have opened their Gallery during the Winter and Spring for the Sale of any Works of History or Landscape painting which may be worthy of admission. Our artists are no longer entirely confined to portrait painting, but they have some, though inadequate encouragement to exert their talents in the higher branches of Art'.

The avowed aim of the British Institution was reasonably enough patriotic—the country was engaged in the greatest war Europe had known at that time—'to remove prejudice against British Arts and British Artists'. But Jane treated this with her customary levity in the presence of would-be serious art and declared 'my preference for Men & Women always inclines me to attend more to the company than to the sight'.

And many will cheer her on!

1813

THE NEXT extant letter from Jane in London is two years later, May 1813. She had stayed with Henry a few weeks earlier to nurse his wife through the terminal days of a long and painful illness and had gone back to Chawton to recover. Henry, in need of company and conversation, drove down to collect his favourite sister and back to Sloane Street in his curricle, the equivalent of a Ferrari. The journey, this time through Guildford, was greatly enjoyed, 'I thought it particularly pretty around Painshill', but that remarkable landscape, developed 40 years earlier, evoked no further response. 'It was about ¼ past 6 when we reached this house, a 12 hour Business', a daunting contrast to today's one and half hours that even a small, clapped-out car takes without exceeding the speed limit. The first few days were quiet. Henry was in mourning for the obligatory minimum of a month, the house brimming with memories of Eliza. 'The quietness does me good.'

The weather was poor and Jane managed only two local visits, one to Mrs Hoblyn further south along Sloane Street, and the second literally round the corner, to see Charlotte Craven, the daughter of a family friend. This young girl was at boarding school at 22 Hans Place, an establishment elegant both in its furnishings and the appearance of its pupils. The school was run by Dominique St Quintin, son of the owner of the Abbey School in Reading that Jane had attended between spring 1785 and Christmas 1786. But there was no attempt to claim former acquaintance, time was short 'only a few minutes to sit with Charlotte Craven' and perhaps reviving an acquaintance after a quarter of a century would have been awkward or boring. At all events, 'I saw no one but Charlotte, which pleased me best'.

Another letter, written four days later, shows the expected adrenalin rush: Jane with two published novels under her belt and the second briefly highly fashionable, is on the move. She is going shopping, she is seeing people—or avoiding them with the pardonable excuse of a trip to Hampstead, that is the churchyard on the hill, at the end of the present Church Row.

Barely a month earlier Eliza had been buried in the same grave as her mother and her son by her first marriage, in the churchyard of St John's. It is a very attractive church, consecrated in 1747, its bricks weathered to a rich terra-cotta and the plain interior with the customary period gallery running along three sides. The only decoration is a fine coat-of-arms of George II, gold glittering against the pale background.

The churchyard overlooks Hampstead, which in 1813 was still a village quite distinct from London, surrounded by open country and overarched by painterly skies: Constable is buried only a few yards away from Eliza. (In the late twentieth century, with trees grown tall, ivy and brambles running amok, many graves are now vague green hummocks.) Bird song by day, foxes at dusk, it was a dreamy scene, encouraging all the obvious quotations from the Romantic poets to fire off in the memory, much like Anne Elliot, on the walk to Winthrop, 'repeating to herself some few of the thousand poetical descriptions extant of the autumn'.

Whatever Jane thought on the occasion, it had served to avoid meeting Miss Burdett: 'If I am a wild Beast I cannot help it. It is not my fault', which is not a prescient comment on genetics but irritation that the knowledge of her authorship of *Sense and Sensibility* and *Pride and Prejudice* was seeping out.

However the glow of having two novels published (*Pride and Prejudice* had come out in January and was selling very well) was with her when she went with Henry to the Exhibition by the Society of Painters in Oil and Watercolours in Spring Gardens, near Charing Cross, a street otherwise noted for having the Spring Gardens Coffee House:

> 'Frequented mostly by gentleman of the army. Good dinners, beds and every accommodation necessary.'

Entry cost to the exhibition cost 1/- to include the catalogue, which quoted prices 'without frames'. It was an annual event, showing the usual mix of Welsh scenery by Cox, Oxford colleges, a few farmyard genre scenes, P.H. Rogers' 'West View of Saltram, the seat of the Rt Hon Lord Boringdon' (who chose Henry in his next incarnation as clergyman, to be the family chaplain) and of course portraits: a fine one by Lawrence of Lt. Gen. the Hon Charles Stuart (now in the National Portrait Gallery), a miniature by Mary Green of Queen Adelaide when Duchess of Clarence.

Did the miniature particularly appeal, like the one of Philip V of Spain in the d'Antraigues' house two years earlier? There was another by J.F.H. Huet-Villiers, who a few years back had distinguished himself in the genre by painting Frederica, Duchess of York. Jane's eye was caught by a young woman 'in a white gown with green ornaments'. Without doubt, this was the portrait of Mrs Bingley, 'excessively like her, size, shaped face, features, sweetness'. Evidently Jane Austen had distinct ideas—not shared with her readers but probably discussed with Cassandra—about how her characters looked. And here, serendipitously, a painter had vividly evoked one of them. If one was so faithfully rendered, why not others? The hunt was on for the portrait of Mrs Darcy—fun!

Private collections were unlikely to be productive, although the Dukes of Devonshire and Northumberland, as befitted their wealth and status, used their London houses to show to vetted visitors parts of their magnificent holdings, in the same way as these days, paying visitors can enjoy them at Chatsworth or Alnwick. Mr J.J. Angerstein, lately retired from a business career that had earned him a stupendous fortune, now had full scope for his 'princely munificence and private generosity', and showed his pictures in his house at 100 Pall Mall; they are good enough for 38 of them to have formed the nucleus of the National Gallery.

Richard Payne Knight, the theoretician of the picturesque, understandably specialised in Salvator Rosa, and his intending visitors were reassured that 'from having long resided abroad he is particularly attentive to foreigners'—hardly an enticement for Jane

Austen who famously limits her novels to the southern half of England. This left the 'Exhibition', that is the Royal Academy in Somerset House, which again aimed at high art, as distinct from the Spring Gardens show earlier in the week, that went for popular recognition of subject and scenes. Finding no Mrs Darcy in the RA they went on to the British Institution, which had a retrospective of Joshua Reynolds.

> 'The First Summer Exhibition contained One hundred and forty three of the best Works of Sir Joshua Reynolds, contributed by seventy-one proprietors, many of them being portraits of their ancestors.'

This combination of patriotism, art and snobbery was very successful. Starting in late April 1813, with a partial re-hang a few weeks later due to other proprietors clamouring to have their ancestors included, it ended in August. Throughout it included the portrait of Mrs Siddons as *The Tragic Muse*, which, despite her interest in actors, evoked no comment from Jane Austen, only a sigh that again she found no portrait of Mrs Darcy. She accounted for her disappointment plausibly enough:

> 'I can only imagine that Mr D. prizes any Picture of her too much to like it should be exposed to the public eye.—I can imagine he wd have that sort of feeling—that mixture of Love, Pride & Delicacy.'

This is probably something of a joke between herself and Cassandra; we know the two of them, and later their nieces, talked about the lives of her characters outside the covers of the books, rather like modern readers avid for prequels, sequels and parallel stories. Or it may have been an attempt to prolong the happiness of that book and carry it, like a talisman, in to the haziness of the future.

Now Henry was on the move: without Eliza the house in Sloane Street was too large and expensive (£11. 13*s*. 4*d* annually for the Poor Rate alone—his partner James Tilson, a family man, paid only £6 round the corner in Hans Place). As a single man, often away from home, Henry needed no space for entertaining. Besides his wife's income, from a trust fund set up for her by her godfather, Warren Hastings, had ended with her life. So it made sense to scale down, and fortunately the bank premises, Austen, Maunde, Austen and Tilson in Henrietta Street, Covent Garden, had space that could be re-vamped into private accommodation to suit Henry's new bachelor status. The work was put in hand. There remained the lease of 64 Sloane Street to dispose of (not far short of 50 years left) and Henry was asking either 500 guineas or a commensurate quarterly rent.

On Sunday morning Henry and Jane went to Belgrave Chapel, new and fashionable with an imposing Doric portico (the architect Smirke had travelled extensively in Italy and Greece). It stood on the corner of Halkin Street and Belgrave Square, on the site of the present Caledonian Club. Then it was behind Knightsbridge Barracks; it was a sign that the Grosvenor Estate was about to start developing the area between Hyde Park Corner and Sloane Street, then mostly open country crossed by several footpaths. Two days later the return to Chawton in Henry's curricle was to take a roundabout tourist route through the gentle landscape of the Thames valley, Windsor, Henley, Reading for the night. Was it a thank you to Jane for having comforted Eliza's last days or Henry in search of an unexceptionable pleasure? For siblings who always got on well, it must have been a pleasant jaunt.

Jane's next London letter is written in September 1813, from Henrietta Street. Again she is staying with Henry (who seems to have off-loaded his house in Sloane Street), and was settled in the living quarters above the bank. Henrietta Street is on the south side of the Covent Garden piazza, more graceful in Jane Austen's day than ours, since it was the piazza designed by Inigo Jones in the late seventeenth century, a continuous arcade of houses 'fitt for the habitations of gentlemen and men of ability'. By 1732 it was fully developed and bringing in a tidy income. At its west end was the church of St Paul (now the actors' church):

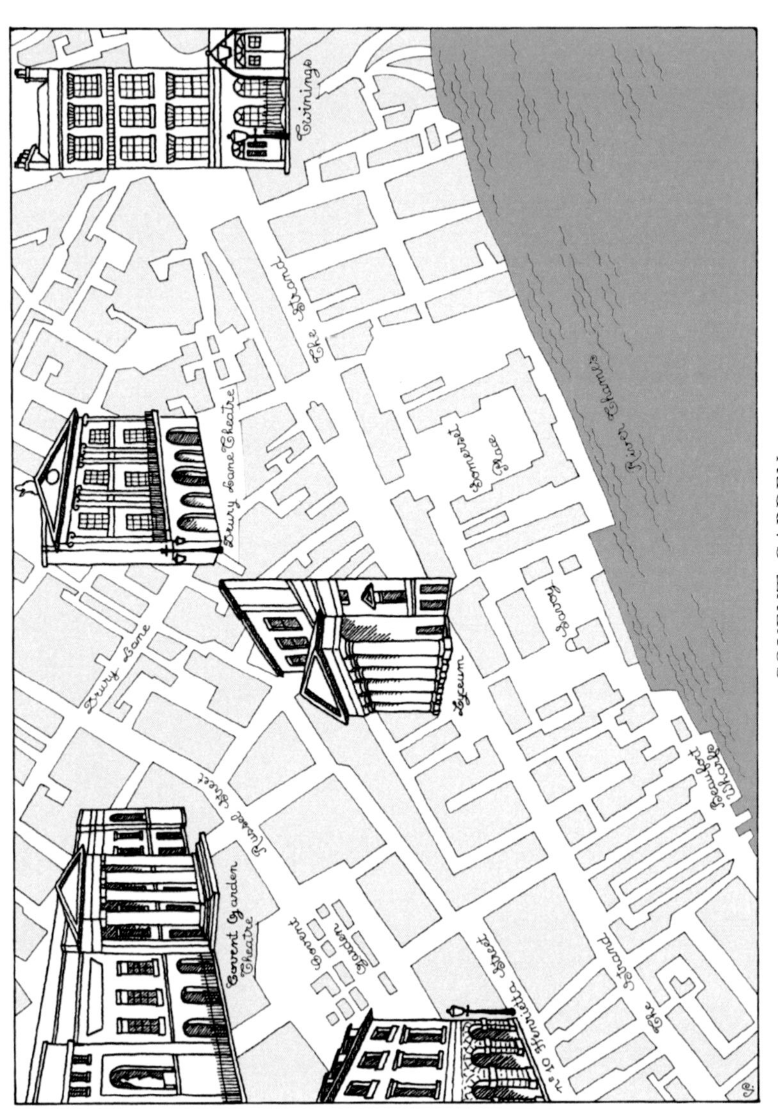

COVENT GARDEN

> 'is a beautiful specimen of its kind. It is so simple in its structure that in fact it is little more than an ornamental barn, but the effect is very pleasing.'

The church is now enhanced by a well-kept and much appreciated garden and 10 Henrietta Street was directly opposite a narrow passage leading to it. The central open space of the piazza, then as now, was occupied by two parallel rows of retail outlets: four separate blocks 14 ft wide in the north row, nearer Long Acre, and three, 21ft wide in the south row. Period ground plans show the lay-out and the names of the lessees and their wares, for instance: 'Earthenware shop Carr'. Access to the retail units was from either north or south, each had a strategically sited fire-place, so that up to four units could share one chimney stack. All the blocks were roofed with steeply pitched tiles. The wide space between the units had only one building on its eastern edge, variously tavern or coffee house. In both cases a licence was needed.

In the north-east corner of the arcaded piazza, where the back entrance to the Opera House now baffles the unwary with a revolving door which stops if touched, was the entrance to number 14, another coffee house described in the period directories as 'under the piazza'. This was the Bedford Coffeehouse:

> 'A truly genteel coffeehouse, where the best accommodation is to be met with.'

Its other more enticing claim to fame was that it had been for many years the hub for the critical reception of plays. From it critics and wits would sally forth to Covent Garden or Drury Lane, the only premises licensed to put on plays from the autumn to late spring; after the performance the party would return, sometimes with the actors, to praise or damn the play.

The influence of the Bedford's denizens was sufficiently well-known to be satirised by Henry Fielding, novelist and dramatist. By 1813 its power was somewhat diluted but it remained a pre-eminent part of the coffeehouse culture, where regulars and strangers could discuss, apart from the arts, business, politics or the current gossip. Everyone was polite and talked in reasoned tones on the issues of the day.

In this egalitarian setting, frequented by politicians, noblemen and merchants, professional men had the impression that their opinions mattered, and even if they did not, it was the best place for networking. As such it is the entirely plausible venue for a young man on the make, like John Thorpe in *Northanger Abbey* to have allegedly often met General Tilney, a much older man of assured social status. General Tilney may indeed have called in at the Bedford whenever business or pleasure brought him to London. Besides, the Covent Garden area, and especially the Strand, was still the obvious place to pick up a girl. The trade was not as blatant as earlier in the eighteenth century, when a coffeehouse sign showing a woman's arm and hand holding a coffeepot denoted that it doubled as a brothel. Such was the Bedford in the 1740s, when its proprietor, William Coburn, held a licence that also allowed him to 'let rooms to tenants', in other words prostitutes. By 1813, with three theatres (Theatre Royal Covent Garden, Theatre Royal Drury Lane and the Lyceum) within a stone's throw, the whiff of dissipation still lingered and the Exeter Exchange added an outlandish note.

On the site of the present Strand Palace Hotel, the Exeter Exchange was a building originally of small shops intended for hosiers, milliners, drapers, an early mini shopping mall, with offices above. But Edward Cross the entrepreneur had taken over the ground floor and established a menagerie with monkeys, lions, tigers, a more exotic hippo and a sloth, and, most popular of all, a five ton elephant named Chunee. Since neither Regent's Park nor the Zoo yet existed, the Exeter Exchange drew a great many visitors, including in *Sense and Sensibility* John and Fanny Dashwood, intent on giving their Harry a treat.

The Covent Garden area, including Henrietta Street, was residentially less desirable than Sloane Street, but in another way the move benefited Henry. As a private banker he was ideally expected to live 'at least the greater part of the year at his banking house—punctual in his hours of business and always found at his desk'. This persona should have been further buttressed by 'serious manners, plain apparel, the steadiest conduct and rigid observance of the formalities'. West End banks, such as Henry's, provided banking services to the gentry and aristocracy (City partnerships, being more aggressive, dealt with mercantile business). So over and above the essential trustworthiness and competence, the partners needed urbane qualities and discretion to attract clients and to present 'an ostensible pattern to society of probity, exactness, frugality and decorum' to retain them. If the move to Henrietta Street showed Henry to be more seriously committed to his work, no harm at all was done.

In fact Henry and his partner Henry Maunde had moved into 10 Henrietta Street, part of the Duke of Bedford's estate, on Lady Day 1808, but the back-dated 21 year lease was signed only on 24 November 1808. The time gap was caused by the third signatory and partner, Frank Austen, the older of the two sailor brothers, being away on active service. Clearly having a naval captain as a partner added—apart from a little money—prestige and patriotic gloss to the enterprise. The signatures were witnessed by the Rev. James Austen, rector of Steventon, that is the eldest brother, and one of his near neighbours, the Rev. George Lefroy, rector of Ashe and widower of 'Madam' Lefroy, Jane's friend and mentor, and uncle of Tom Lefroy, the erstwhile boy friend.

The lease 'in consideration of Repairs' including 'maintenance of the Pump for the water-closet' involved a yearly rent of £110, payable quarterly and insurance for £2000 in the Sun Fire Office, where plans of streets and individual houses were kept. In the exquisitely kept accounts of Daniel Beaumont 'of a Rate in lieu of Rectors Rate payable to his Grace the Duke of Bedford' Henry and his partners were shown as paying the rent punctually, actively using the premises (that is there was no sub-letting) together with an additional partner, one Jas. Tilson. This was the Mr Tilson who had a house in Hans Place, near Henry's former home in Sloane Street, and whose wife was frequently visited by Jane Austen, either alone or with her niece Fanny.

Now in September 1813 not only Jane but also Fanny and two younger sisters, Marianne and Lizzy, were staying in Henrietta Street. Looking at a plan and allowing space for the bank's business, it looks as if there were three bedrooms, plus a dressing room for Jane and Fanny, who shared a bed—a bit of a squash by modern standards, but Jane found it very snug and comfortable. Edward Knight, the girls' father, lodged in a nearby hotel. He had brought the girls to London to go to the dentist, Mr Spence in Bond Street, 'dentist to his Majesty' no less, and for some recuperative retail therapy and theatre going.

In the years that Jane Austen visited London there were four licensed theatres: the theatres Royal of Covent Garden and Drury Lane for dramatic performances during the normal season from autumn to late spring. In summer, as Lydia Bennet pertly informs her sisters, the Little Theatre in Haymarket, (nearly on the site of the present Theatre Royal) was licensed to put on regular drama. Across the road from it, on the site of the present Her Majesty's, was the King's Theatre, the only theatre in London licensed to perform Italian opera. 1811 saw a production of *Così fan tutte*, not a draw for Jane who preferred her music 'at a pleasant distance'. Of the unlicensed theatres the Lyceum, roughly on its present site, was the best supported and together with the two theatres royal, in Bow Street and Drury Lane, a five minute stroll away from Henrietta Street.

Theoretically Jane, with her long-standing pleasure in dramatic performance, should have rejoiced to be in the thick of it, not that she says so. Although she went to the theatre each time she was staying with Henry, she did not always get to the performances she particularly wanted to see; seats in boxes were sold out (the gentry did not sit on the benches in the pit, least of all its ladies), performances were swapped round at the last minute. As far as we know she never made it to *King John* with Mrs Siddons as Constance, who was by all reports stunningly impressive in the part bringing the whole audience to tears with the understated expression of grief over her dead son. Possibly the acclamation that greeted her interpretation of the part was nourished by the experience of similar loss among many in her audience: the war, though far from total in the twentieth century sense, still exacted casualties at sea and especially in the Peninsula, where British Forces, largely under the command of Wellington, had been so successfully involved against the army of Napoleonic France.

Generally actors were judged by their ability to generate emotions in the audience, making plays with scenes of pathos or distress popular (hence *King John*), at the expense of political or more cerebral plays like *Julius Caesar*. In serious plays actors wore hybrid costume, inspired by classical sculpture, as in Reynolds' portrait of Mrs Siddons as *The Tragic Muse*. For comic parts contemporary dress was worn, with the actresses vying to out-do each other, turning themselves into elegant clothes-horses they were referred to as 'women of fashion'. Considering how much space Jane's London letters give to fashion total absence of comment on this aspect of theatre is surprising. Perhaps it was left for conversation on return to Chawton, where reports of the latest ideas would be appreciated by the village ladies, rather like Mrs Bennet who was 'very glad to hear what' the London-based Mrs Gardiner has 'to tell us of long sleeves'.

Another aspect of theatre, 'decorations', that is scenery, evokes no comment either. Yet this had become one of the strengths of the London stage while Garrick was manager of Drury Lane (1747-1776) and employing Philip de Loutherbourg as his scene designer. De Loutherbourg had come from France, where he had made a name for himself as a painter of pastoral landscapes and decorous marine scenes. Having sized up what was on offer in London he wrote a memo to Garrick saying that if co-operation was to continue he, Loutherbourg, wanted control over costume (it was the time when in Paris also authenticity of costume was sought) and significant influence over dance and music. In other words Louth-erbourg was after an integrated production, and Garrick, busy modernising Drury Lane from style of acting to stage lighting, was happy to give him his head.

The result was a series of 'decorations' for a variety of shows (some of which the Austen siblings later performed in the barn at Steventon) which transformed the way plays were not only staged but also criticised. Newspapers took to praising, or not, the painterly back-cloths. Loutherbourg's work was a huge success, culminating in *The Wonders of Derbyshire* a spectacular with eleven scene changes, for which he had spent the autumn in Derbyshire painting on the spot.

Decorations thus became a significant part of the capital of a theatre, and the practice of the set transporting the audience to a different world and enhancing the mood and action became the norm—totally ignored by Jane. But a rare allusion to paintings that she allows herself is in Elizabeth Bennet's visit to Pemberley. The tour of the house includes the picture gallery which held:

> 'many good paintings, but Elizabeth knew nothing of the art; and from such as had already been visible below, she had willingly turned to look at some drawings of Miss Darcy, in crayons, whose subjects were usually more interesting and also more intelligible'.

Which left the plays, in the plural. Each evening would consist of three pieces, generally two plays, one of which could be a melodrama, with a musical interlude, sometimes a ballet. It made for a very long evening and it was accepted that all the audience could not be present for the whole of the three pieces. People arrived late or left early, since the three pieces could not be equally interesting. Ideally seats were in 'the stage box', a box literally on the edge of the apron abutting the proscenium arch—great for seeing the actors' faces, though they might reasonably object to the audience conversing while they were declaiming. The modern habit of polite, if not rapt attention was a much later development. Jane's young nieces were likely to be absorbed, but the adults chatted comfortably. This was normal practice, witness the scene in *Pride and Prejudice*, when Elizabeth Bennet has a long conversation with her aunt during a performance. Boxes were mostly larger than modern ones, with seats available in the first, second or third row. Drury Lane had five rows of boxes, the Little Theatre three; audiences were vociferous in their approval or condemnation, so the evening could turn out to be noisier than the actors intended.

On the first evening the family party went to Covent Garden for *Don Juan*, a pantomime, 'the last of three musical things whom we left in Hell at ½ past 11'. The next evening was the *Clandestine Marriage* (by Coleman and Garrick, one of the latter's greatest comic successes, better known these days in Cimarosa's operatic version), *Five Hours to Brighton*, a forgettable play written two years earlier and *The Beehive*, an adaptation into a musical farce of one of Kotzebue's over-numerous plays. A good time was had by all, even if Jane's pleasure was distinctly moderate. But she was the aunt-on-duty and theatre going was more agreeable than traipsing round shops after her nieces (Fanny was a determined shopper) or accompanying them to 21 Old Bond Street to Mr Spence, the King's dentist and hearing 'each of two hasty Screams'. Before the end of September she was with them at Godmersham, writing to her brother Frank about the girls' visit to London and expressing her dissatisfaction with the standard of acting:

> 'There was no Actor worth naming—I believe the Theatres are thought at a low ebb at present.'

1814

BARELY six months later, in 1814, with *Emma* underway and the proofs of *Mansfield Park* being corrected, Jane was back in London. Again Henry had come to collect her, the journey was done in comfort with a break for the night at Cobham, they reached Henrietta Street 'considerably before 2'. One of the bank employees met them and 'in reply to enquiries after News said that Peace was generally expected'. The allied armies were on French soil and although Napoleon was contriving to inflict minor defeats on the separate national forces, he had lost in Russia too many men, horses and ordnance to project any immediate serious threat. The heads of the allied governments had set up in Chatillon-sur-Seine, some 120 miles south east of Paris in fine burgundy country, not that any good wine was locally available, which no doubt added to their discomfort, irritation and inability to agree on what to do next. However peace was coming after twenty-one weary years and would sooner rather than later bring Frank and Charles, the sailor brothers, back to safety and half pay, and with them a great many others. Peace would also rapidly cut government spending. A collapse of wages and prices was on the horizon. If Jane and Henry thought and talked in these terms (and Henry as a banker should have worked out the sequence) not a word reached Cassandra in Jane's March letters. Her niece Fanny also came to town, so as usual the days were filled with visitors, shopping and the theatre.

Except that first Jane sent 'Miss P's two letters to the twopenny post'. This was a small kindness to a neighbour: carrying the letter from Hampshire to London and then entrusting it to the local twopenny post was cheaper and quicker than the normal mail service. The London post had risen to 2*d* in 1801 (this was part of additional taxation to pay for the war), to be paid in advance, deliveries were to individual houses (three times a day in Chelsea) and several collections, the last one at 8 p.m. This was the means used by

Marianne Dashwood while staying with Mrs Jennings near Portman Square and trying to contact the faithless Willoughby. This postal service was most satisfactory.

As was Jane's opinion of Edmund Kean as Shylock: 'I cannot imagine better acting', but she had reservations about Miss Smith as Portia and the other 'parts were ill-filled and the Play heavy'. This was an in-built weakness of the star system; audiences went to see what the star actor made of a well-known part, and to the educated Shakespeare was very well known, as Henry Crawford and Edmund Bertram agree in *Mansfield Park*. Which left the other parts more or less to chance or convention. There were recognised stage postures designed to reveal fear, hope, sincerity, etc. The dynamic of speech and telling gesture was choreographed so that, for instance, Mrs Siddons as Lady Macbeth had her practised gestures and whoops of voice in the 'out damned spot' scene. Garrick as Hamlet had used a much imitated 'start' at seeing the ghost. Similarly Darcy 'starts' when he is rejected at Hunsford, again on meeting Elizabeth at Pemberley and yet again in the inn at Lambton. Marianne Dashwood has her theatrical scream on discovering Willoughby's perfidy. Edward Ferrars' stammering is part of the recognised rhetoric of sincerity. These made for instant recognition of the character's emotion at particular points in the plot, either on the stage or in print.

The other stage shows seen were less pleasing: *Nourjahad*, a melodramatic spectacle, with Ellisten one of Jane's favourite actors, familiar from her theatre-going in Bath, miscast 'not at all calculated for his powers'. She expected to be amused by *The Devil to Pay*, starring Dora Jordan (mistress of the future William IV) in one of her most successful comic parts and bored by that old warhorse *Artaxerxes*, an opera by Thomas Arne, of *Rule Britannia* fame. When first staged in 1762 *Artaxerxes* had been a spectacular, with so many special effects that the price of tickets had to be raised, leading to riots both inside and outside the theatre. The highly acclaimed soprano, Miss Stephens, left her cold since 'Miss S. is a pleasing person and no skill in acting'. To judge by her likeness in the National Portrait Gallery, Miss Stephens was a beautiful brunette. Her sweet soprano voice was ideal for the part of Mandane. Leigh Hunt, the critic, essayist and friend of the Romantic poets, describes her 'like nothing else on the stage' for the natural 'naiveté of her manner' and 'the stream of delicious sound' she produced. Notwithstanding she was a down to earth girl, married the elderly Earl of Essex and survived him by forty-two years. But on this night in 1814 Jane Austen disregards Miss Stephens' musical talents, which 'gave me no pleasure . . . being what Nature has made me on that article'.

Did the ramifications of the operatic score bore her? Did she like only short, simple melodies, like the songs copied into her music book? She can scarcely have been tone-deaf since at Chawton she played the piano daily before breakfast. Why bother? Just to keep her hand in to play dance music for her nieces? With twentieth century hindsight, was it a way of gearing up for the day's writing, giving an airing to the right-half of the brain before putting to work the language centres on the left? Be that as it may, she liked Miss Stephens no better the following night in *The Farmer's Wife* 'a Musical thing in 3 Acts'. Songs had been added to a comedy by Charles Coffey which provided good parts for Mathews, the tall, thin comic star, Liston playing the traditional cunning London servant and Emery his ignorant Yorkshire counterpart—they provided genuine entertainment.

In between theatre going, planning how to refresh her wardrobe, worrying about a lawsuit her brother Edward was involved in, she reported Henry's reactions to *Mansfield Park* that she was then proofreading. 'He found the last half of the last volume extremely interesting', which she took at face value and rapidly moved on to Twinings, the tea merchants at 216 the Strand. Even today, with traffic surging up from Waterloo Bridge and swinging round the Aldwych, the restored shop with its delicate aroma of tea is barely ten minutes' walk from Henrietta Street. Cassandra was expected, the sisters hoped to overlap briefly in Henrietta Street and to go to Covent Garden. There the resident star had been J.P. Kemble (brother of Mrs Siddons), a classical actor specialising in parts calling for nobility of character, so Hamlet and Coriolanus showed him at his best. His successor, Charles Mayne Young, was a not altogether satisfactory replacement in that vein, and now was going head to head with Drury Lane's Edmund Kean of 'the impassioned delivery', as Richard III.

Within the month Napoleon had abdicated and in another fortnight shipped off to Elba. Amid general rejoicing the Prince Regent's unpopularity persisted, and yet his support had been unswerving for successive prime ministers pursuing the long war against France. Later generations owe him also for the playful architectural extravaganza, the Brighton Pavilion; his enthusiasm for the formation of the National Gallery; his gift of his father's library to the British Museum (now Library); his active interest in all the arts and his splendid collections—which of course cost a great deal of money.

There was also the question of his unfortunate marriage and a general impression of laxity at court, in current jargon, sleaze. Besides, the war, although successful, had just about bankrupted the country, much like WWII. Taxation had risen enormously ('Whenever you see an object, tax it' was not altogether a joke) and the highly productive new-fangled income tax showed no sign of being repealed. What to do?

Let's have a party! In other words invite the allied sovereigns to London to celebrate and hope that some of the remarkable popularity of the Tsar Alexander would rub off on Prinny. They came. Wherever he went, the Tsar was cheered to the echo ('Take care of yourself and do not be trampled to death running after the Emperor' wrote Jane on 14 June to Cassandra still in London) and he snubbed Prinny whenever he could. The whole party went to Portsmouth for a naval review and were entertained at Petworth. 'I long to know what this Bow of the Prince's will produce' adds Jane in the same letter, not knowing that Castlereagh, the Foreign Secretary, had already secured the chief British gains.

The allied sovereigns left, but the parties went on. On 22 June 1814 White's, the club with the best façade in St James's Street, gave a ball for 2000 and Henry was one of the guests. It was his social apogee ('What a Henry!' laughed Jane) and it seems to have gone to his head. For he promptly moved out of snug, cheap to run, on the spot for work Henrietta Street and back to leafy, expensive Hans Town. This time it was a corner house, 22 Hans Place, with a large garden and direct view of the entrance front of Henry Holland's elegant Pavilion. With hindsight the disadvantages of the move are obvious: at a crucial time for his business Henry was taking his eye off the ball. He, the senior partner, was moving away from the hub of news and conversation half way between Westminster and the City and was therefore that much less likely to hear from either of anything that might affect his trade. Then the new house was expensive: the Poor Rate alone was £3. 15*s*. 0*d* a quarter, a live-in maid was needed, the garden had to be looked after. Strangest of all, Henry's move to Hans Place followed closely his obtaining the lease of 63 Sloane Street, that is the house next to his former one; he hung on to it till 1822, a full six years after being declared bankrupt, all the while forking out punctually £3 a quarter for Poor Rate. There is no evidence of any sort of suggest why he bought this lease, or what the house was used for, so, dear reader, you are free to 'give a loose to your fancy' with ideas from wild to sober.

In August Jane made her own way to London. Henry, who had been enjoying himself at the Canterbury races, met her and picking one of the four hackneys in the coach company yard, took her to Hans Place, 'a darling place', she found 'the Garden is quite a love' and chose for herself the front attic, presumably for its view of the central greenery and the movement of people to and from the surrounding houses. As to visitors, life was fairly quiet, which did not stop Jane from having a very close look at what was worn at 'Mrs

Latouche's, where dress is a good deal attended to'. She noticed that petticoats were short, a development considered positively indecent in a party of English visitors to Geneva in the summer of 1814. *Mansfield Park*, which had been advertised for 9 May, was selling steadily even without reviews, so Jane had every prospect of more than covering her costs (she had published it at her own expense, Egerton was handling only the printing and sales); any profit, eventually amounting to £350, would be added to the safe and patriotic haven she had chosen, Navy Bonds.

Jane had time to write to her friend Martha Lloyd, and the letter is unusual in two respects. First it contains Jane's only recorded opinion of specific paintings, Benjamin West's *Healing in the Temple* and his *Rejection by the Elders*. The latter 'is the first representation of our Saviour which has ever at all contented me'—again she is after the literal representation of face and figure to express the personality, no other elements of the painting have any impact. Secondly she reports Henry's views on the political situation, that is the continuing war with America started in 1812 (the treaty ending it was still three months in the future). They are wholly downbeat: this unwinnable war is 'what will ruin us'. Which makes Henry's move to an expensive house the more puzzling.

Jane was back at Hans Place in November 1814 and took the opportunity of visiting her newly-married niece Anna Lefroy in Hendon. This short journey could have been done by local coach, but since Jane was travelling with her rich brother Edward, a hackney may have taken them in greater comfort, as well as waited before returning them.

In the evening, with the addition of Henry, they went to Covent Garden to see its new star, Miss O'Neill in *Isabella*. This had been one of Mrs Siddons' most impressive roles, as the devoted wife and mother who, believing herself widowed, is talked into re-marriage, only to find her adored husband very much alive. Jane went armed with 'two Pocket handkerchiefs', for Miss O'Neill had the reputation of reducing her audience to sighs and tears. Jane was not, she remained coolly analytical and the handkerchiefs unused. There was a date with Egerton, her publisher in Whitehall, about the possibility of a second edition of *Mansfield Park*. Egerton's speciality was 'Military Library' and with the end of hostilities, many accounts of the campaigns in the Peninsula, Russia, Germany were expected to come his way. Understandably he demurred so *Mansfield Park* in its second, much corrected but not-so-successful edition was published by Murray, Byron's publisher, only in February 1816.

Jane had time for one more visit, to her brother Charles and his family. This involved going to Keppel Street, now in the thick of the university district, then one of the streets radiating out of the modern squares built to provide the professional middle classes with clean air and quietness. Keppel Street is just a little stroll from Brunswick Square, home of John and Isabella Knightley, minor figures in *Emma*, still being written at the time. Isabella is stout in her defence of Brunswick Square:

> 'We are so very airy I should be unwilling, I own, to live in any other part of the town: there is hardly any other I would be satisfied to have my children in: but we are so remarkably airy!'

And so it was and remains, because it abuts Coram Fields, the large open area that housed the Foundling Hospital, on the other side of which is Mecklenburg Square, with thick green hedges and trees, its east side a beautiful terrace of fine houses. Beyond were the open fields to Hampstead. The Foundling Hospital, decorated by Hogarth and comforted by Handel's music, was for many years London's favourite charity, its chapel the preferred Sunday venue for citizens with an active social conscience, Charles Dickens for one. It is wholly appropriate that Isabella Knightley, who fusses endlessly about her children's health, should have been housed in the one spot in the capital well-known for many years for its generous care of abandoned children.

1815

THE WAR with the infant United States was over, *Emma* finished by the end of March 1815, while Napoleon, escaped from Elba, was having a last shot at regaining his empire. The navy was at full stretch again, taking British troops to the United Provinces. The suspense lasted until 21 June, when news of the victory at Waterloo reached the Prince Regent and his Foreign Secretary, Castlereagh. 'Normal' life could resume, with its usual load of difficulties.

The first for Jane Austen, who started *Persuasion* in August, was to find a publisher for *Emma*. Murray, Byron's publisher, 'a Rogue, but a civil one', strung her along but eventually agreed to publish on commission. Jane was staying in Hans Place, enjoying the weather 'The 17th of October and summer still!' and the usual flow of visitors. Suddenly, Henry got ill, 'something bilious but chiefly Inflammatory', took to his bed and Mr Haden, 'the apothecary from the corner of Sloane Street' was called in.

'A young man said to be clever', Charles Thomas Haden had studied in Edinburgh and London and been elected FRCS at 22, the youngest ever. He went to Paris to study French techniques and on his return in 1814 introduced the stethoscope, even more of a novelty than the slide-rule Jane's brother Edward had bought himself the year before. Mr Haden set up in 62 Sloane Street and devoted a good portion of his time to the Chelsea, Brompton and Belgrave Dispensary in Sloane Square. This had been started in 1812, partly through the efforts of William Wilberforce, with the aim of helping 'the sick poor—not paupers—the delivery of married women in their own homes and attention to the diseases of women and children'. In its first year of operation it relieved 1200 patients. Of course Mr Haden had to have lucrative private patients also and was 'certainly very attentive'. His competence was very calming, and Jane went on to describe the usual flow of visitors, actual and potential, as she sat in Henry's room 'working' (i.e. correcting proofs) 'or writing' (letters or *Persuasion*).

Henry was a model patient, did exactly as he was told, but his condition deteriorated and Jane, in alarm, summoned the siblings to his bedside. James, Edward and Cassandra arrived hurriedly and Henry's life hung in the balance. Mr Haden called in a colleague for a second opinion, most likely Dr Matthew Baillie, who had treated Henry during a much earlier bout of chest trouble. Luckily, a few days later Henry turned the corner, James and Edward returned home, leaving the sisters to gentle Henry into full recovery and wonder at an unexpected development: Dr Baillie was one of the Prince Regent's physicians and told him of Jane's presence in London. It turned out that the Prince Regent had read and greatly enjoyed her novels to date and as a sign of his admiration instructed his librarian, the Rev. James Stanier Clarke, to invite her to Carlton House and show her the library. An invitation from the effective monarch could not be refused, especially when given in such a flattering manner, for Mr Clarke called in Hans Place to deliver it, as had Mr Bingley in *Pride and Prejudice*, to invite the Bennet family to his ball. Jane had to swallow her unequivocal dislike of the Prince Regent and go.

One reason for Jane's long-standing dislike of the Prince Regent was his treatment of his wife:

> 'I shall support her as long as I can, because she is a Woman & because I hate her Husband'.

The marriage had been forced on the Prince (he ensured it was conditional on having his enormous debts paid and a large increase to his income) and he retaliated by sending his then mistress, Lady Jersey, to Greenwich to welcome his bride on her arrival from Germany.

From the start there were faults on both sides, which Lady Jersey found it easy to exploit. Soon enough the row became official, involving Parliament. The newspapers, pamphleteers and caricaturists cashed in, the crowd took sides (mostly for the Princess of

Wales) and the Prince denied his wife access to their daughter. The outraged Princess of Wales took herself to the Continent, to more scandal and Jane wrote:

> '. . . the Princess, I am resolved at least always to think that she would have been respectable, if the Prince had behaved only tolerably by her first'.

But a royal wish is a command, so on 13 November 1815 Jane went to Carlton House, the official residence of the Prince Regent. She left no account of this visit, no description of the place—Henry Holland's simple dignified building 'overdone with finery' thought Robert Smirke, the austere architect of the Belgrave Chapel familiar to Jane — no comments on the books. The whole exercise must have caused some difficulty in keeping a straight face. For a start Mr Clarke was Mr Collins writ large, the Prince Regent being his Lady Catherine de Burgh. Further he had literary ambitions and insufficient talent to support them. He lacked the sophistication to cope with the dissolute life of the court as much as he lacked the gumption to condemn it.

Mr Clarke was incompetent and idle at coping with the parishes allocated to him and he had the effrontery to tell Jane Austen what to write. Conventionally enough, he first explained that her next book should be dedicated to the Prince Regent, and, hilariously, *Emma* is indeed dedicated to the rakish Prinny. Mr Clarke then wanted her to write a novel about a clergyman, clearly based on his own life. (Jane incorporated his hints into her spoof *Plan of a Novel.*) And finally, with the royal wedding in the offing, he thought 'a Historical Romance illustrative of the History of the august house of Coburg' into which Princess Charlotte, daughter of the Prince Regent was marrying—should be Jane's next book. Both suggestions were politely and firmly declined.

Fortunately there were sources of genuine satisfaction. Henry's health recovered slowly and his convalescence was cheered by loans of books from Murray and Mr Haden, who was found to be a treasure, 'something between a Man and an Angel'. He called repeatedly, he was expected to dinner ('There's Happiness!') he came and 'brought good Manners and clever conversation', books were lent, borrowed, he met Jane's niece Fanny—in London officially to help her aunt with the invalid, in fact to shop and have music lessons. Fanny also liked Mr Haden, his only defect that without a pianoforte for accompaniment he refused to sing although known to be accomplished in the art. The sentences about him have the high spirits and flutter of expectant happiness familiar from Jane's earliest letters about her flirtation with Tom Lefroy. Was her heart having a fantasy holiday? After all she was two months into *Persuasion* with its theme of a late-flowering love.

Aunt and niece went to the Belgrave Chapel, shopping to 'the miseries of Grafton House', met a few people, received game sent from Godmersham and Jane organised her washing: 'I will not send any more dirty Linen—it will not answer when Carriage is to be paid each way'. The reason for not having her laundry done in London, apart from price, was the quality of the water. Thames water was generally used; the river being polluted the clothes emerged clean after a fashion but distinctly smelly, with the odour lingering despite repeated washings in clean well-water.

Although Mr Haden would not sign off his patient, Henry was venturing into the garden every day. He wanted to go to Oxford before Christmas, presumably as part of his duties as Receiver General for Taxes, in other words a 'tax farmer'. This antiquated system of collecting taxes then prevalent in much of Europe was open to abuse and had been one of the popular grievances that had led to the French revolution. In England, to obtain the position of Receiver General the appropriate candidate—apart from character and competence—had to lay down a surety of £30,000, which Henry had borrowed from his rich relations: his uncle James Leigh Perrot and his brother Edward of Godmersham Park. The government, desperate to pay off various war loans, was acting on a report of a parliamentary committee, which had discovered that some tax collectors held on to a quarter's public money till the following quarter day. For bankers this was not blatantly illegal, but using public money for their own business was. It was tempting, since Henry's bank had suffered a number of bad debts. Also it had opened branches in Alton and Petersfield backed by money from local tradesmen.

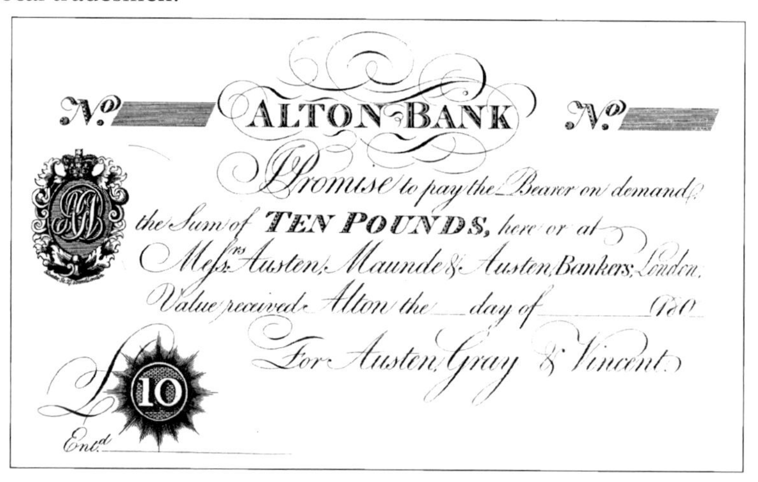

On the strength of this, the bank had issued a number of small denomination bank notes which sooner or later had to be redeemed by gold or, at a pinch, silver. The weak point in this sequence was that, with the end of hostilities in 1815 government orders for supplies suddenly plummeted and tradesmen lost their main customer almost from one day to the next. Bankruptcy for Henry and his partner James Tilson, in the next house but one in Hans Place, was on the horizon, as it was for many other small country banks.

Jane alludes to this in a letter of 2 December 1815. By now *Emma* was in print. It remained to ask John Murray to send a set to Carlton House and for Jane to send another to the Countess of Morley, whose husband would shortly ease Henry's reduced circumstances by appointing him his private chaplain. Books borrowed from Mr Haden were returned with a note 'I leave Town early on Saturday and must say 'Good bye' to you'.

Whatever emotion that stark polite note covered could be channelled into *Persuasion*.

Jane, stoical, self-controlled, was taking her last leave of London, the city that always gave her a heightened sense of being alive, and of the man whose temperament, intelligence, manners seemingly fitted the template for her elusive Mr Right.

She returned to Chawton, wrote teasing letters to her nephew and nieces, mentioned the weather (1816 was 'the year without a summer') rather than her health. She died nineteen months later, and we, her readers and admirers, know her scarcely better for this visit to the London of her day.

Acknowledgements

All aspects of Jane Austen's life have been raked over many times. For a newcomer to the field the difficulty lies as much in clearing the head of previous theories as of finding something new to say. However three books, apart from the novels and letters, have been relied on:

Jane Austen, a Family Record: W. Austen-Leigh, R.A. Austen-Leigh, Deirdre Le Faye, (The British Library 1997) with its very handy chronology.

Jane Austen, Her Life: Park Honan, (Max Press 2007) for the scope and depth of its scholarship and the excellence of its index.

Rites of Peace: Adam Zamoyski, (Bloomsbury 2007) for the detailed historical context.

Local detail came from the London Metropolitan Archive and the library of the of the London Society. More detail came from the Guildhall Library, the National Arts Library, the Royal Borough of Kensington and Chelsea Library, Local Studies section, the Westminster Archive Library.

Anthony Finney allowed one item from his collections to be reproduced and Stephen Twining offered the watercolour of the shop in the Strand. The archivists of the Bedford, Cadogan and Grosvenor Estates were prompt, patient and informative; David Le Lay, Chairman of the Chelsea Society, gave a private seminar on Henry Holland's building methods; Jean Aylward shared her information about furniture shops, Helen Lefroy the results of her research into Lord Morley's family, and Jill Manasseh her guile in navigating Google.

John Hunter, a non-Austenite, read the whole MS and made astute suggestions and Susan Close worked her usual magic, turning a mass of paper into a legible text. I am again indebted to Veronique Avon-Yapp for drawing the splendid maps. To all of them, and to friends who gave time, sympathy and alcohol, my thanks.

V.Q.